やさしい英語で読む
アンデルセン童話

Contents

目次

学習法	05
本書の利用法	06
おやゆび姫 *Thumbelina*	08
王様とナイチンゲール *The Emperor and the Nightingale*	18

人魚姫
The little Mermaid — 28

モミの木
The Fir Tree — 38

マッチ売りの少女
The Little Match Girl — 48

デイジー
The Daisy — 58

お姫様とエンドウ豆
The Princess and the Pea — 68

ワイルドスワン
The Wild Swans — 78

かがり針
The Darning Needle — 88

ブリキの兵隊
The Hardy Tin Soldier — 98

INDEX
108

学習法

本書を使って英語の読解力や聴解力をアップさせるのに有効な学習法を紹介します。
お話を楽しみながら、英語力を上げるのに役立ててください。

Step1
Vocabulary をヒントにしながら物語を読む

↓

Step2
日本語訳で確認

↓

Step3
CD（英語）を本を見ながら聞く

↓

Step4
CD（英語）を本を見ないで聞く

CD.2

偶数トラックには英語で、奇数トラックには日本語で、
お話が収録されています。
用途に合わせて、CD を活用してください。

本書の利用法

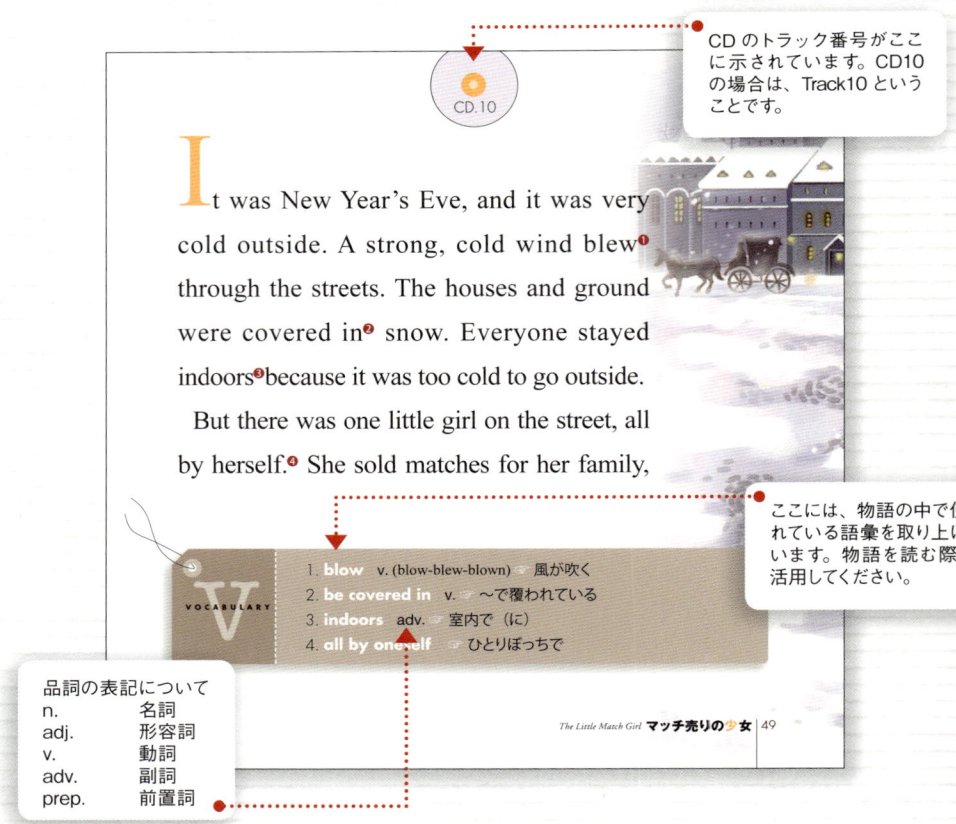

CDのトラック番号がここに示されています。CD10の場合は、Track10ということです。

It was New Year's Eve, and it was very cold outside. A strong, cold wind blew[1] through the streets. The houses and ground were covered in[2] snow. Everyone stayed indoors[3] because it was too cold to go outside.

But there was one little girl on the street, all by herself.[4] She sold matches for her family,

VOCABULARY

1. **blow** v. (blow-blew-blown) 風が吹く
2. **be covered in** v. ～で覆われている
3. **indoors** adv. 室内で (に)
4. **all by oneself** ひとりぼっちで

ここには、物語の中で使われている語彙を取り上げています。物語を読む際に活用してください。

The Little Match Girl **マッチ売りの少女** | 49

品詞の表記について
n. 名詞
adj. 形容詞
v. 動詞
adv. 副詞
prep. 前置詞

▶ **本書は、誰もが知っているアンデルセン童話 10 話を収録しています。
1 つのお話はイラストや日本語訳を含めて 10 ページで構成されており、
手軽に読み進めることができます。**

各お話の最後には日本語訳が見開きで載っています。日本語だけを読んでも自然なように、英語を意訳したものもありますので、必ずしも Vocabulary で紹介された意味と一致するとは限りません。

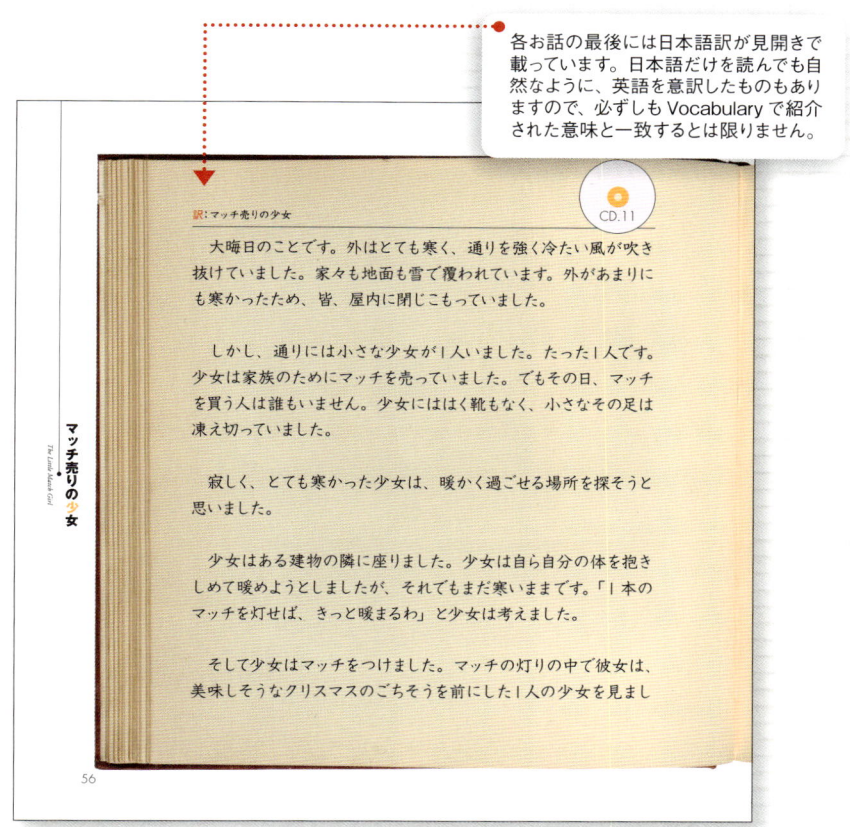

おやゆび姫

Thumbelina

There was once a woman who wanted a child, so she went to a fairy❶ for help. "Here is a seed," said the fairy. "If you plant it in a pot,❷ your wish will come true."

The woman did what she was told. In time, a beautiful flower grew. When the flower opened, the woman saw a tiny❸ girl sitting in it!

This made the woman very happy. "I will name you Thumbelina," she said, "because you are no bigger than my thumb!" She loved her daughter very much.

One day, an ugly❹ toad❺ saw Thumbelina. "She would make a good wife for my son," thought the toad.

VOCABULARY

1. **fairy** n. ☞ 妖精
2. **pot** n. ☞ 植木鉢
3. **tiny** adj. ☞ とても小さい
4. **ugly** adj. ☞ みにくい
5. **toad** n. ☞ ヒキガエル

The toad stole Thumbelina and took her to a pond.❶

Luckily, a kind fish helped Thumbelina get away.❷ After that, Thumbelina met a mouse. "If you cook and clean for

me, you can stay with me," he said.

Thumbelina agreed and was living happily with the mouse. Then one day, the mouse told her she had to marry his friend, a mole.❸ Thumbelina didn't care for the mole, but she had no choice.

Before the wedding, Thumbelina found a sick bird. She looked after❹ the bird until he was healthy again. In return for❺ her kindness, the bird offered to take her away.

VOCABULARY
1. **pond** n. ☞ 池
2. **get away** v. ☞ 逃げる
3. **mole** n. ☞ モグラ
4. **look after** v. ☞ 〜の世話をする
5. **in return for** ☞ 〜に対するお礼として

As they flew, they saw a pretty white flower. "I can be happy living there," said Thumbelina.

When they reached the flower, Thumbelina was surprised. A very small man was standing in the flower. "I am the king of❶ flowers," he said. "Marry me and be my queen." Thumbelina said yes and they lived happily ever after.

VOCABULARY

1. **the king of ~**　☞ ～の王

訳:おやゆび姫

　昔々、ある女性がいました。彼女は子どもがほしかったので、助けを求めに妖精のもとを訪れました。「ここに種があります」と妖精は言いました。「これを鉢に植えれば、願いは叶うでしょう」

　女性は言われた通りにしました。やがて美しい花が育ちました。花が開くと、そこに小さな少女が座っています！

　女性はすっかりうれしくなってしまいました。「あなたをおやゆび姫と名付けましょう」。女性は言いました。「私の親指ほどの大きさなんですもの！」と。女性は娘にたくさんの愛情を注ぎました。

　ある日、みにくいヒキガエルがおやゆび姫を見かけました。「私の息子のよい嫁になるだろう」とヒキガエルは考えました。そしておやゆび姫をさらい、池に連れていきました。

　幸運なことに、親切な魚に助けられておやゆび姫は逃げることができました。その後、おやゆび姫はネズミに会いました。「僕のために料理と掃除をしてくれたら、一緒にいてもいいよ」とネズミ

は言いました。

　おやゆび姫は同意してネズミと一緒に幸せに暮らしました。そしてある日、ネズミは、自分の友だちであるモグラと結婚するよう言いました。おやゆび姫はモグラが嫌いでしたが、結婚するよりほかありませんでした。

　結婚式を前に、おやゆび姫は病気の鳥を見つけます。おやゆび姫は鳥が元気になるまで世話をしました。その親切のお返しに、鳥はおやゆび姫を連れ出すことを申し出ました。

　空を飛んでいるとき、彼らは美しい白い花を見かけました。「あそこなら幸せに暮らせるわ」とおやゆび姫は言いました。

　花のところに到着したおやゆび姫は驚きました。花の中にとても小さな男性が立っていたのです。「僕は花の王です」とその男性は言いました。「僕と結婚して妃になってください」。おやゆび姫は「はい」と答え、それからずっと幸せに暮らしました。

王様とナイチンゲール

The Emperor and the Nightingale

There was once an emperor who loved beautiful things. One day, he read about the music of the nightingale. The book said that nothing was lovelier❶ than the nightingale's song.

The emperor sent some men into the forest to find the nightingale. When they returned, the emperor was disappointed. The nightingale was just a plain,❷ brown

1. **lovelier** adj. ☞ より愛らしい [原級：lovely]
2. **plain** adj. ☞ 地味な

bird. Then she began to sing. Her song was so beautiful that it brought tears to the emperor's eyes.❶

"Lovely nightingale," he said, "I

must give you a gift. What do you wish for?"

"You gave me enough already," said the nightingale. "I saw tears in

VOCABULARY

1. **bring tears to one's eyes** ☞ 目に涙を浮かべる

an emperor's eyes. That is enough."

The nightingale remained[1] with the emperor and sang for him each night. One day, though, someone sent the emperor a box. Inside the box was a mechanical[2] nightingale.

The new nightingale sang just like[3] the real one, but it was covered with[4] colorful1 jewels. When it sang, its tail

VOCABULARY

1. **remain** v. ☞ とどまる
2. **mechanical** adj. ☞ 機械の
3. **just like** ☞ 〜と同様に、まるで〜のようで
4. **be covered with** v. ☞ 〜で覆われている
5. **shine** v. (shine-shone-shone) 輝く

moved and the jewels shone.❺ The emperor was pleased with this gift, and he sent the real nightingale back to the forest.

The mechanical nightingale sang beautifully day and night. One day, though, it stopped working. The emperor was very sad. He became sick, and everyone thought he would die.

"If I could hear the nightingale again, I would get better," said the emperor. Suddenly, he heard some marvelous❶ music. The real nightingale was singing at his window.

Her song cured[2] him, and he became strong again.

After that day, the emperor treasured[3] the real nightingale. He put away[4] the mechanical bird and never looked at it again.

VOCABULARY

1. **marvelous** adj. ☞ すばらしい
2. **cure** v. ☞ 治す
3. **treasure** v. ☞ 〜を大切にする
4. **put away** v. ☞ 片付ける

The Emperor and the Nightingale **王様とナイチンゲール**

訳：王様とナイチンゲール

　昔々、美しいものが大好きな王様がいました。ある日、王様はナイチンゲールの声について書かれた本を読みました。その本には、ナイチンゲールの歌声ほど愛らしいものはないと書かれていました。

　王様は家来たちを森に送り、ナイチンゲールを探させました。彼らが戻ってきたとき、王様はがっかりしてしまいました。ナイチンゲールが、さえない茶色い鳥だったからです。しかし歌い始めると、その歌声はあまりにも美しく、王様の目には涙があふれました。

　「愛らしいナイチンゲールよ」と王様は言いました。「お前に贈り物をあげよう。何がほしい」

　「もう十分にいただいています」とナイチンゲールは言いました。「王様の目に涙が浮かぶのを見ました。それで十分です」

　ナイチンゲールは王様のもとにとどまり、毎夜、王様のために歌いました。ところが、ある日、何者かが王様に1つの箱を送りました。箱の中に入っていたのは機械仕掛けのナイチンゲールでした。

新しいナイチンゲールの歌声は本物そっくり。おまけにそれは色とりどりの宝石に彩られていました。歌うと尾が動き、宝石が輝きます。王様はこの贈り物に喜び、本物のナイチンゲールを森に帰してしまいました。

　機械仕掛けのナイチンゲールは昼も夜も美しく歌いました。しかしある日、壊れてしまいます。王様はとても悲しみ、病気になってしまいました。皆、王様は死んでしまうのではないかと考えました。

「もう一度、ナイチンゲールの歌声が聴けたら元気になるんだが」と王様は言いました。すると突然、すばらしい歌声が聞こえてきました。本物のナイチンゲールが窓際で歌っていたのです。その歌声は王様を癒し、王様は再び元気になりました。

　その日以来、王様は本物のナイチンゲールを大切にしました。機械仕掛けの鳥は片付けてしまい、２度と目にすることはありませんでした。

The Little Mermaid
人魚姫

Deep in the ocean, there lived a Sea King and his people.❶ The Sea King had six beautiful daughters. His youngest daughter, Ariel, was the most beautiful of all.

Ariel's greatest wish was to see the world above the sea. One night, Ariel swam to the surface of the water and saw a large ship. Among the men aboard,❷ she spotted a very handsome man who was a prince.

Suddenly, a big storm came. The huge③ waves made the ship tip over. Ariel brought the drowning prince to shore and sang sweetly to him. As he was waking up, Ariel swam away.

Back at home, Ariel sought④ help from the Sea Witch. "This potion⑤ will make you become human," said the Sea Witch. "In return, I desire your beautiful voice." Using magic, she put Ariel's voice into a shell.⑥

VOCABULARY

1. **one's people** n. ☞ 家来、部下
2. **aboard** adv. ☞ [船に] 乗って
3. **huge** adj. ☞ 大きな
4. **seek** v. (seek-sought-sought) ☞ 求める、依頼する
5. **potion** n. ☞ 薬
6. **shell** n. ☞ 貝

Ariel swallowed① the potion and passed out.② She woke up on land, with her prince looking at her. "Are you alright?" he asked. Ariel had no voice to answer him.

The prince brought Ariel to his castle. One day, he told her, "My heart belongs to③ the woman who saved my life." Ariel couldn't tell him it was her.

One day, the prince decided to marry a princess from a distant④ land. This broke Ariel's heart. When she saw the

VOCABULARY

1. **swallow** v. ☞ 〜を飲み込む
2. **pass out** v. ☞ 気絶する、意識を失う
3. **belong to** v. ☞ 〜の所有物である
4. **distant** adj. ☞ 遠い

princess, Ariel knew it was the Sea Witch!

Ariel feared for❶ the prince. She had to fight the Sea Witch to prevent❷ the wedding. During the fight, the Sea Witch's shell broke, which gave Ariel her voice back. As Ariel spoke aloud,❸ the prince realized she was the one who had saved him.

Turning to Ariel, he said, "It was you all along."❹ The prince kissed Ariel, and she knew she would be with him forever.

VOCABULARY

1. **fear for** v. ☞ （人）のことを心配する
2. **prevent** v. ☞ 防ぐ、とめる
3. **aloud** adv. ☞ 声を出して
4. **all along** ☞ 最初からずっと

訳：人魚姫

　海深くに、海の王様と家来たちが住んでいました。海の王様には、6人の美しい娘がいましたが、なかでも末娘のアリエルが最も美しい娘でした。

　アリエルの一番の夢は、海の上の世界を見ることでした。ある夜、水面まで泳いでいったアリエルは、大きな船を見かけます。そして船上の男たちの中に、とてもハンサムな男性を見つけました。彼は王子でした。

　突然、大きな嵐が来ました。大きな波を受けて船は転覆してしまいました。アリエルは、溺れている王子を岸に引き上げ、彼に向かって愛らしい声で歌いかけました。王子が目を覚ましそうになると、アリエルは泳ぎ去ってしまいました。

　家に戻ったアリエルは、海の魔女に助けを求めました。「この薬を飲めば人間になれる」と海の魔女は言いました。「そのかわり、お前の美しい声をもらうよ」。魔女は魔法を使い、アリエルの声を貝に閉じ込めてしまいました。

　アリエルは薬を飲み込むと気を失ってしまいました。陸で目を覚

ますと、あの王子が見つめています。「大丈夫ですか」と王子は聞きました。アリエルは、それに答える声を持っていません。

王子はアリエルを城に連れて行きました。ある日、王子はアリエルに言います。「僕の心は命を救ってくれた女性のものなのです」。アリエルは、それが自分であることを伝えることができませんでした。

ある日、王子は遠い国からやってきた王女と結婚することを決めました。アリエルは絶望しました。王女を見たとき、アリエルはそれが海の魔女だとわかりました。

アリエルは王子が心配になりました。結婚式を阻止するためには、海の魔女と闘わなければなりませんでした。闘いのさなか、海の魔女の貝が割れ、アリエルに声が戻ってきました。アリエルが大声を上げると、王子は自分を救ってくれたのはアリエルであることに気づきました。

アリエルのほうを向くと、王子は言いました。「君だったんだね」。王子はアリエルにキスをしました。そして、アリエルは永遠に王子と一緒なのだと思ったのです。

The Fir Tree
モミの木

Once there was a short fir tree.❶ It lived in the forest. Every day it felt the warm sun. Every morning, it watched groups of children playing nearby.❷ The tree didn't care. "I wish I were as tall as the other trees," it thought.

Years passed, and the tree grew taller. In the winter, some men cut it down. It was terribly❸ painful, and the tree fainted.❹

VOCABULARY
1. **fir tree** n. ☞ モミの木
2. **nearby** adv. ☞ すぐ近くに
3. **terribly** adv. ☞ ひどく、ものすごく
4. **faint** v. ☞ 気絶する、失神する

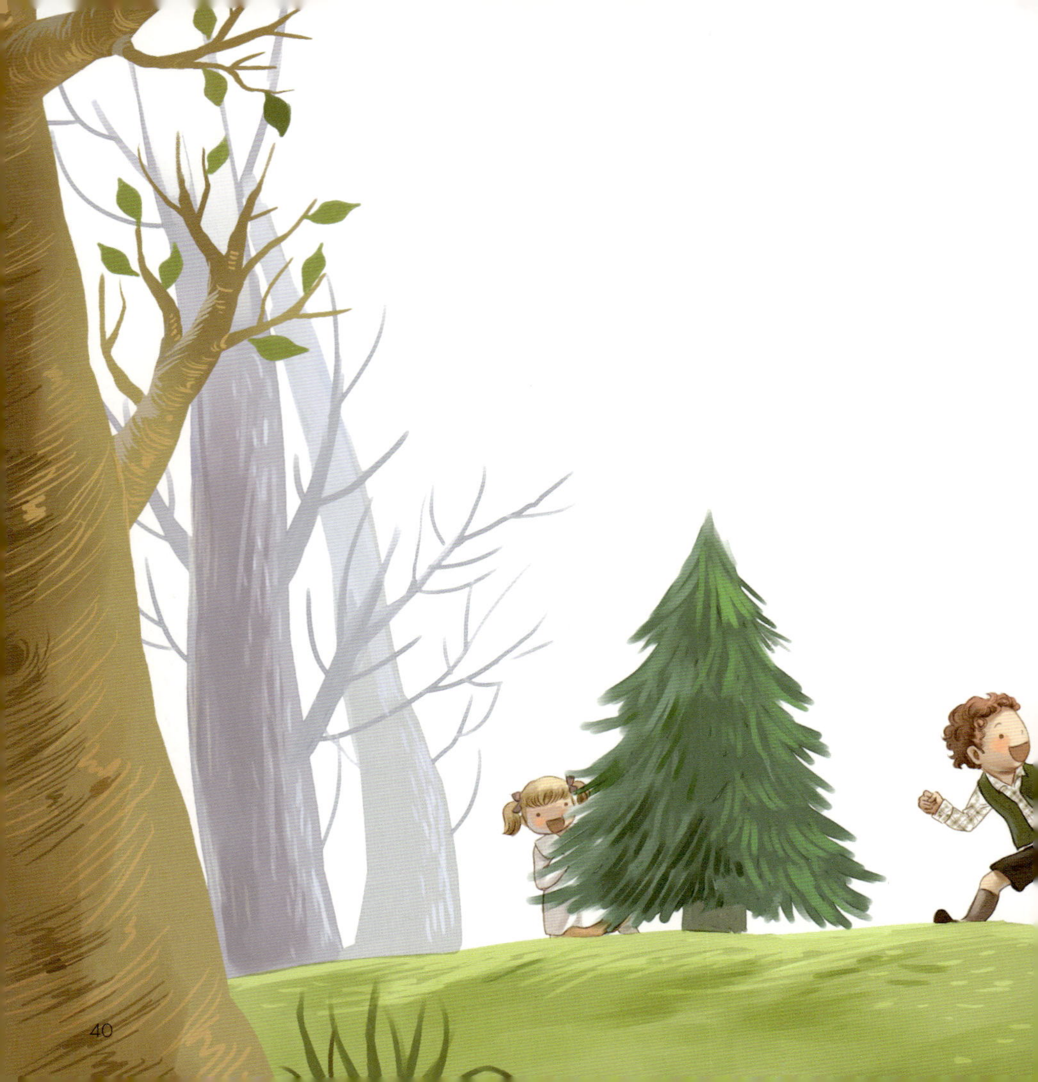

The Fir Tree **モミの木** | 41

When the tree woke up, it was in a living room. Children were placing❶ candles on it. "Where am I?" thought the tree. "Oh, I wish I were back in the forest!"

That evening, children hung❷ silverballs from the tree's branches.❸ A small boy placed a golden star upon the top of the tree. It became very bright and beautiful.

Later on, an old man sat under the tree and told a story.

VOCABULARY
1. **place** v. ☞ 置く、取りつける
2. **hang** v. (hang-hung-hung) ☞ 〜をつるす、〜を掛ける
3. **branch** n. ☞ 枝
4. **decoration** n. ☞ 飾りつけ
5. **upstairs** n. ☞ 2階、上階

The tree listened, and enjoyed the story very much. "Wow," thought the tree. "Things will be even better tomorrow!"

The tree did not think of its gold and silver decorations.❹ It didn't care about the beautiful living room. "Tomorrow," it thought. "Wonderful things will happen to me tomorrow!"

The next day, some men carried the tree to an upstairs❺ room. "Oh!" cried the tree. "It's so lonely here!"

"The forest was warm and comfortable," ❶ thought the tree. "When I was in the living room, I wore beautiful candles! I was happy, but I didn't know it."

A year passed. A man brought the tree down to the garden. "What an ugly old Christmas tree," said the man. He chopped the tree into ❷ small pieces. "I wish I had cherished ❸ my happy times more," thought the tree. But it was too late.

VOCABULARY

1. **comfortable** adj. ☞ 心地良い
2. **chop ~ into** v. ☞ 〜を…に切る
3. **cherish** v. ☞ 〜を大事にする

The Fir Tree **モミの木** | 45

訳：モミの木

　昔々、1本の背の低いモミの木がいました。その木は森の中で暮らしていました。毎日、モミの木は暖かい太陽を感じ、毎朝、近くで子どもたちの一団が遊んでいるのを見ていました。でも、そんなことには関心がありませんでした。「他の木々のように背が高ければいいのに」とモミの木は思いました。

　何年かが過ぎ、木の背丈は伸びました。冬、男たちが木を切り倒してしまいました。ひどく痛かったため、木は気を失ってしまいました。

　目が覚めると、木はリビングルームにいました。子どもたちが木にろうそくを飾っています。「ここはどこ？」と木は考えました。「あぁ、森に帰りたい！」

　その夜、子どもたちは木の枝々に銀の玉を吊るしました。小さな少年が、木のてっぺんに金の星を飾りました。木はとても華やかで美しくなりました。

しばらくして、老人が木の下に座り、物語を語りました。木は耳を傾け、その話を大いに楽しみました。木は思いました。「わぁ、明日はもっと素晴らしい日になる！」

　木は、金や銀の飾りのことは考えていませんでした。美しいリビングルームも気にも留めていませんでした。「明日」と木は思いました。「明日、僕に素晴らしいことが起こるんだ！」

　翌日、男たちが木を２階の部屋に運んでいきました。木は嘆きました。「あぁ、ここはとっても淋しい」

　「森は暖かく気持ちがよかった」と木は思いました。「リビングルームにいるとき、僕は美しいろうそくをまとっていた！　僕は幸せだった。でもそれに気づいていなかったんだ」

　何年かが過ぎ、１人の男が木を庭に下ろしました。「なんて醜くて古いクリスマスツリーなんだ」と男は言い、小さな木片に切り刻んでしまいました。「幸せな時間をもっと大切にすればよかった」と木は思いました。でも、すべては遅すぎたのです。

マッチ売りの少女

The Little Match Girl

It was New Year's Eve, and it was very cold outside. A strong, cold wind blew❶ through the streets. The houses and ground were covered in❷ snow. Everyone stayed indoors❸because it was too cold to go outside.

But there was one little girl on the street, all by herself.❹ She sold matches for her family,

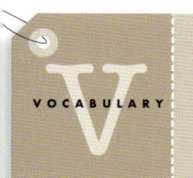

> **VOCABULARY**
> 1. **blow** v. (blow-blew-blown) ☞ 風が吹く
> 2. **be covered in** v. ☞ 〜で覆われている
> 3. **indoors** adv. ☞ 室内で（に）
> 4. **all by oneself** ☞ ひとりぼっちで

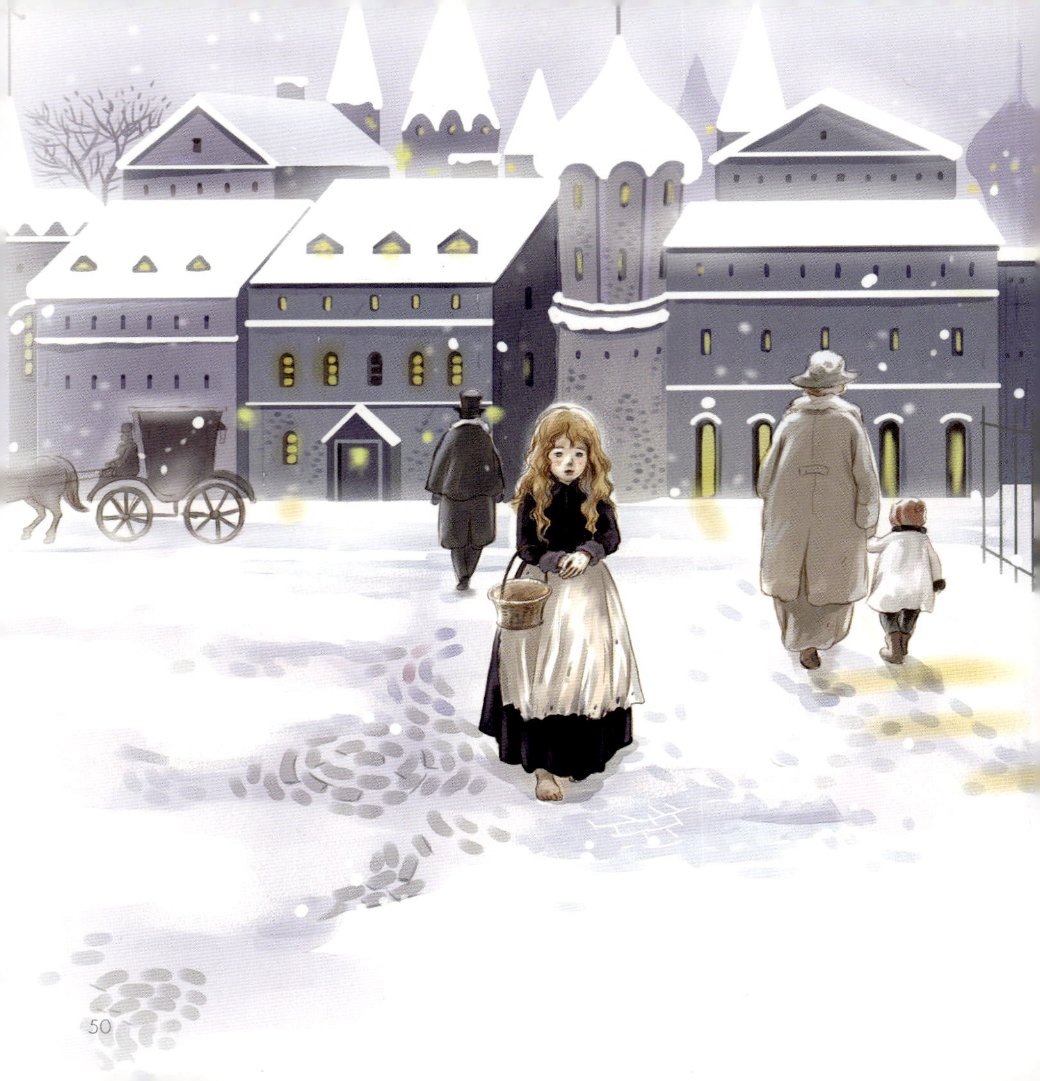

but that day nobody had bought any. She had no shoes, and her tiny feet were frozen.

The little girl felt lonely and very cold, so she decided to find a place to stay warm.

The little girl sat down next to a building. She hugged herself❶ to stay warm,❷ but it was still too cold. "If I light one match, maybe I can keep warm," she thought.

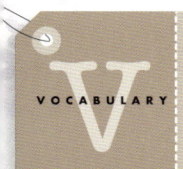

VOCABULARY

1. **hug oneself**　v. ☞ ［寒さで］体を縮こめる、自分を抱きしめる
2. **stay warm**　v. ☞ 暖かくして過ごす

So the girl lit❶ a match. In the light, she saw a little girl preparing❷ to eat a delicious❸ Christmas dinner. After the first match went out, she lit another one. This time, she saw a beautiful Christmas tree.

When the girl lit another match she saw her grandmother, even though her grandmother had died a long time ago.❹

"Please," said the little girl. "Don't go, grandmother. I am so sad and lonely here." The little girl did not want

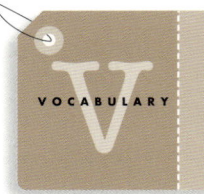

VOCABULARY

1. **light** v. (light-lit-lit) ☞ 〜に火をつける
2. **prepare** v. ☞ 用意する、〜を準備する
3. **delicious** adj. ☞ おいしい
4. **a long time ago** ☞ ずっと昔に、昔

The Little Match Girl **マッチ売りの少女** | 53

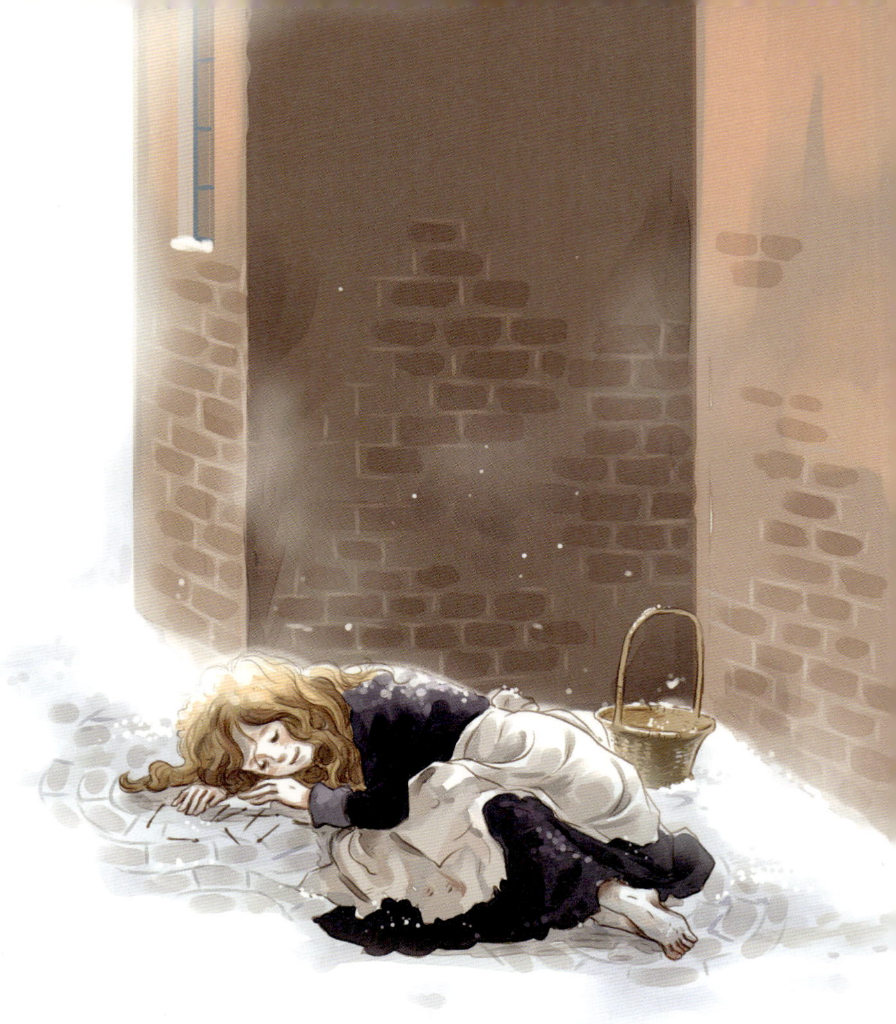

her grandmother to leave, so she lit all of her matches together.❶

Her grandmother smiled, and looked very kind. She hugged the little girl. Together they flew❷ high in the sky.❸ It was so free and wonderful that the little girl laughed.

The next morning, people found a little girl, who had died in the snow. Nobody knew the beautiful things she had seen, or how happy she was, with her grandmother.

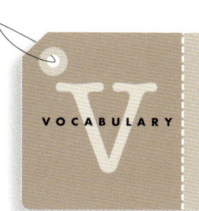

VOCABULARY

1. **together** adv. ☞ 一緒に
2. **fly** v. (fly-flew-flown) ☞ 飛ぶ
3. **high in the sky** ☞ 空高く、はるか上空に

訳：マッチ売りの少女

　大晦日のことです。外はとても寒く、通りを強く冷たい風が吹き抜けていました。家々も地面も雪で覆われています。外があまりにも寒かったため、皆、屋内に閉じこもっていました。

　しかし、通りには小さな少女が1人いました。たった1人です。少女は家族のためにマッチを売っていました。でもその日、マッチを買う人は誰もいません。少女にははく靴もなく、小さなその足は凍え切っていました。

　寂しく、とても寒かった少女は、暖かく過ごせる場所を探そうと思いました。

　少女はある建物の隣に座りました。少女は自ら自分の体を抱きしめて暖めようとしましたが、それでもまだ寒いままです。「1本のマッチを灯せば、きっと暖まるわ」と少女は考えました。

　そして少女はマッチをつけました。マッチの灯りの中で彼女は、美味しそうなクリスマスのごちそうを前にした1人の少女を見まし

た。最初のマッチが消えると、もう1本マッチをすりました。今度は、美しいクリスマスツリーが見えました。

　もう1本マッチをすると、とうの昔に亡くなったおばあさんの姿が見えました。

　「お願い」と少女は言いました。「行かないで、おばあさん。ここはとてもさみしくて、ひとりぼっちなの」。少女はおばあさんにいてほしくて、残りのマッチをすべて同時に灯しました。

　微笑んだおばあさんは、とてもやさしそうに見えました。おばあさんは少女を抱きしめ、2人は一緒に空高く飛んで行きました。あまりにも自由で気分がよかったので、少女は笑い声を上げました。

　翌朝、人々は雪の中で息絶えている小さな少女を見つけました。少女が見た美しい光景のことも、少女がおばあさんと一緒でどれほど幸せだったかも、知る人は誰もいません。

The Daisy
デイジー

A little daisy[1] lived in the countryside,[2] next to a small path.[3] Its petals[4] were white, like the snow. Its center was yellow, like the sun.

The daisy was tiny, but it was very happy. Some of the other flowers were taller and more attractive[5] than the daisy. Others were more colorful. However, the daisy was not jealous. All it needed was the warm sun.

The daisy looked up at the sky, and saw a bird flying.

VOCABULARY

1. **daisy** n. ☞ デイジー、ひなぎく
2. **countryside** n. ☞ 田舎
3. **path** n. ☞ 小道
4. **petal** n. ☞ 花びら
5. **attractive** adj. ☞ 魅力的な

"I am so lucky," thought the daisy. "I can feel the sun and see the beautiful sky. I am rich!"

The daisy watched the bird. "He will visit the other flowers," thought the daisy. "They are so beautiful." Instead,[1] the bird came to the daisy and sang to it. The daisy was so pleased.

Later, two boys chased[2] the bird and captured[3] it.

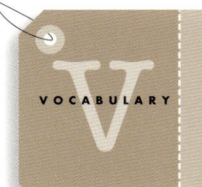

VOCABULARY

1. **instead** adv. ☞ そうしないで、そのかわりに
2. **chase** v. ☞ 〜を追う、追跡する
3. **capture** v. ☞ 捕らえる、捕獲する

The Daisy デイジー | 61

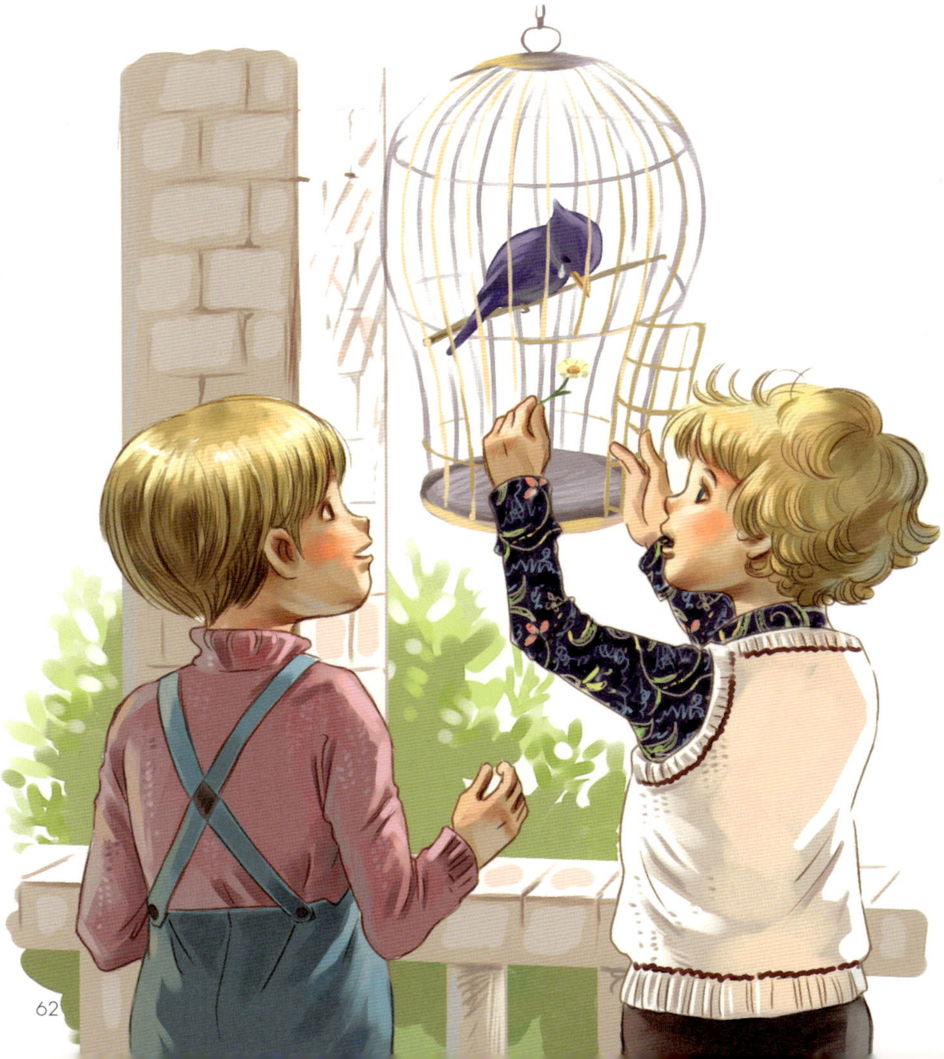

They put it in a cage.❶ "That is such a pity,"❷ thought the daisy. "I wish I could stay with him, and make him feel better."

In the cage, the bird sang sad songs. The boys took the daisy, and put it in the cage.

That night, the careless❸ boys forgot to give the bird water. "I am so thirsty," said the bird. The daisy wanted to comfort❹ him, but it could not move. The bird smiled

VOCABULARY

1. **cage** n. ☞ 鳥かご、ケージ
2. **pity** n. ☞ かわいそうなこと
3. **careless** adj. ☞ 不注意な、うかつな
4. **comfort** v. ☞ 楽にする、安心させる

sadly, and kissed the daisy.

In the morning, the bird was dead. The boys cried, and buried[1] him in a wooden[2] box. They put beautiful flowers by the bird's grave.[3]

The boys threw the daisy onto the path. Nobody remembered the daisy, who had so much concern[4] for the bird, and who tried so hard to help it.

VOCABULARY

1. **bury** v. ☞ 埋める、[遺体を] 葬る
2. **wooden** adj. ☞ 木製の、木でできた
3. **grave** n. ☞ 墓
4. **concern** n. ☞ 気遣い、心配

The Daisy デイジー | 65

訳：デイジー

　田舎の小さな道の脇に、1本の小さなデイジーが咲いていました。花びらは白く、雪のよう。花心は黄色で、太陽のようでした。

　デイジーは小さいけれど、とても幸せでした。デイジーより背が高く魅力的な花たちもいたし、もっとカラフルな花たちもいました。でも、デイジーは嫉妬したりしませんでした。温かい太陽があれば十分だったのです。

　デイジーが空を見上げると、1羽の鳥が飛んでいました。「私はとても幸せだわ」とデイジーは思いました。「太陽を感じることができて、美しい空が見られる。なんて恵まれているのかしら！」

　デイジーは鳥を見つめました。「鳥はほかの花たちのところに行くのね」とデイジーは考えました。「だって、花たちはとても美しいもの」。ところが、その鳥はデイジーのところにやって来て、デイジーに歌いかけました。デイジーはとてもうれしくなりました。

　しばらくすると、2人の少年が鳥を追いかけ、捕まえてしまいま

した。2人は鳥をカゴの中に入れました。「なんてかわいそうなのでしょう」とデイジーは思いました。「鳥さんと一緒にいて、気持ちを楽にしてあげられたらいいのに」

　カゴの中で鳥は悲しい歌を歌いました。少年たちはデイジーを摘み取り、カゴの中に入れました。

　その夜、不注意な少年たちは鳥に水をやるのを忘れてしまいました。「のどがとても渇いた」と鳥は言いました。デイジーは元気づけたかったけれど、動くことができません。鳥は悲しく笑ってデイジーにキスをしました。

　朝、鳥は死んでいました。少年たちは泣き、木箱に鳥を埋葬しました。そして鳥の墓の傍らに美しい花々を供えました。

　少年たちは小道にデイジーを投げ捨ててしまいました。鳥のことをあれほど心配し、あれほど一生懸命に助けようとしたデイジーのことを、誰も覚えていませんでした。

お姫様とエンドウ豆

The Princess and the Pea

There was once a prince who wanted a wife. Many rich and beautiful girls wanted to marry him, but the prince rejected[1] them all. "I will only marry a real princess," he told the queen.

Then one night, there was a terrible[2] storm. In the middle of the storm, a

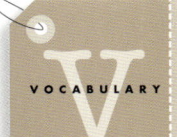

VOCABULARY

1. **reject** v. ☞ 断る、認めない
2. **terrible** adj. ☞ ひどい、極端な

girl knocked on the palace door. "I am a princess," she said, "and I wish to marry the prince."

The prince was doubtful.[1] "She doesn't look like a princess," he said to the queen. "Her hair is a mess,[2] and

VOCABULARY		
1. **doubtful**	adj.	疑わしい、本当とは思えない
2. **mess**	n.	乱雑、ボサボサ

The Princess and the Pea **お姫様とエンドウ豆** | 71

her clothes are covered with mud. Besides, princesses don't wander around[1] in a storm."

"Leave it to me," said the queen. "I will find out if she is a real princess." And she invited the girl to spend the night at the palace.

The queen herself prepared a bed for the girl. She went into the bedroom and put a pea[2] under the mattress.[3] Then she put nineteen very soft mattresses on top.[4] When she

VOCABULARY

1. **wander around** v. ☞ ウロウロ歩きまわる、ほっつき歩く
2. **pea** n. ☞ エンドウ豆
3. **mattress** n. ☞ マットレス
4. **on top** ☞ 上に

was finished, the bed nearly touched the ceiling!❶

The next morning, the girl looked awful.❷ "What is wrong, dear child?" asked the queen. "Didn't you sleep well?"

"No," complained❸ the girl, "I barely❹ slept at all. There was something hard in the bed, and I tossed and turned❺ all night! Now my whole body is black and blue."❻

The queen smiled and told the prince that he had found his princess. "She felt the pea through twenty

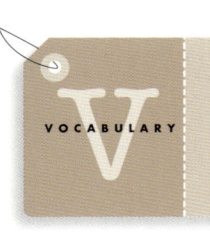

VOCABULARY

1. **ceiling** n. ☞ 天井
2. **awful** adj. ☞ ひどい、嫌な
3. **complain** v. ☞ 文句を言う
4. **barely** adv. ☞ ほとんど〜ない
5. **toss and turn** v. ☞ ゴロゴロと寝返りを打つ
6. **black and blue** adj. ☞ ［人・体の部分が］あざだらけである

mattresses," said the queen. "Only a real princess could be so sensitive."[1] The prince was so happy. He married the princess, and they lived happily ever after.[2]

VOCABULARY

1. **sensitive** adj. ☞ 繊細な
2. **live happily ever after** ☞ 末永く幸せに暮らす

The Princess and the Pea **お姫様とエンドウ豆** | 75

訳：お姫様とエンドウ豆

　昔、お嫁さんを求める王子がいました。多くの金持ちで美しい若い女性たちが王子との結婚を望みましたが、王子はすべて断りました。「正真正銘の王女と結婚したいのです」と王子は王妃に言いました。

　そしてある夜、ひどい嵐が来ました。嵐のさなか、1人の若い女性が王宮の扉をたたきました。「私は王女です」と彼女は言いました。「王子様と結婚がしたいのです」

　王子は疑いました。「彼女は王女には見えない」と王妃に言いました。「髪は乱れているし、服は泥だらけ。何より、王女なら嵐の中をさまよったりしない」

　「私に任せなさい」と王妃は言いました。「彼女が本物の王女かどうか、私が見さだめましょう」。そして王宮で一夜を明かすようその女性を招き入れました。

王妃は女性のために自らベッドを用意しました。王妃は寝室に入り、マットレスの下に豆を入れました。そして、その上にとてもやわらかい 19 枚のマットレスを乗せました。準備を終えたとき、ベッドは天井に届きそうなほどになっていました！

　翌朝、女性はひどい顔色をしていました。「おや、どうしたの？」と王妃は聞きました。「よく眠れなかったのかしら？」

　「はい」と女性は不平を言いました。「ほとんど眠れませんでした。ベッドに何か固い物があって、一晩中寝返りをうっていたのです！だから私の体はあざだらけです」

　王妃は微笑んで、王女を見つけたと王子に伝えました。「彼女は 20 枚のマットレスを通しても豆があることがわかりました」と王妃は言いました。「これほど繊細なのは本物の王女だけです」。王子はとても喜び、王女と結婚してずっと幸せに暮らしました。

The Wild Swans
ワイルドスワン

This is the story of a very far away country. The king and queen of this country had 11 sons and one daughter. Their sons were very handsome.❶ Their only daughter's name was Elisa. One day, the queen passed away.❷

Later, the king found a new wife. However, the new queen was a very bad person. She hated the king's children. She used magic to change the 11 boys into white swans.❸ After that, she made Elisa leave the castle.

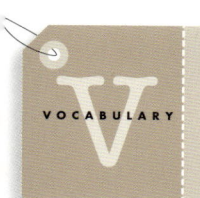

VOCABULARY

1. **handsome** adj. ☞ ハンサムな、顔立ちが美しい
2. **pass away** v. ☞ 亡くなる
3. **swan** n. ☞ 白鳥

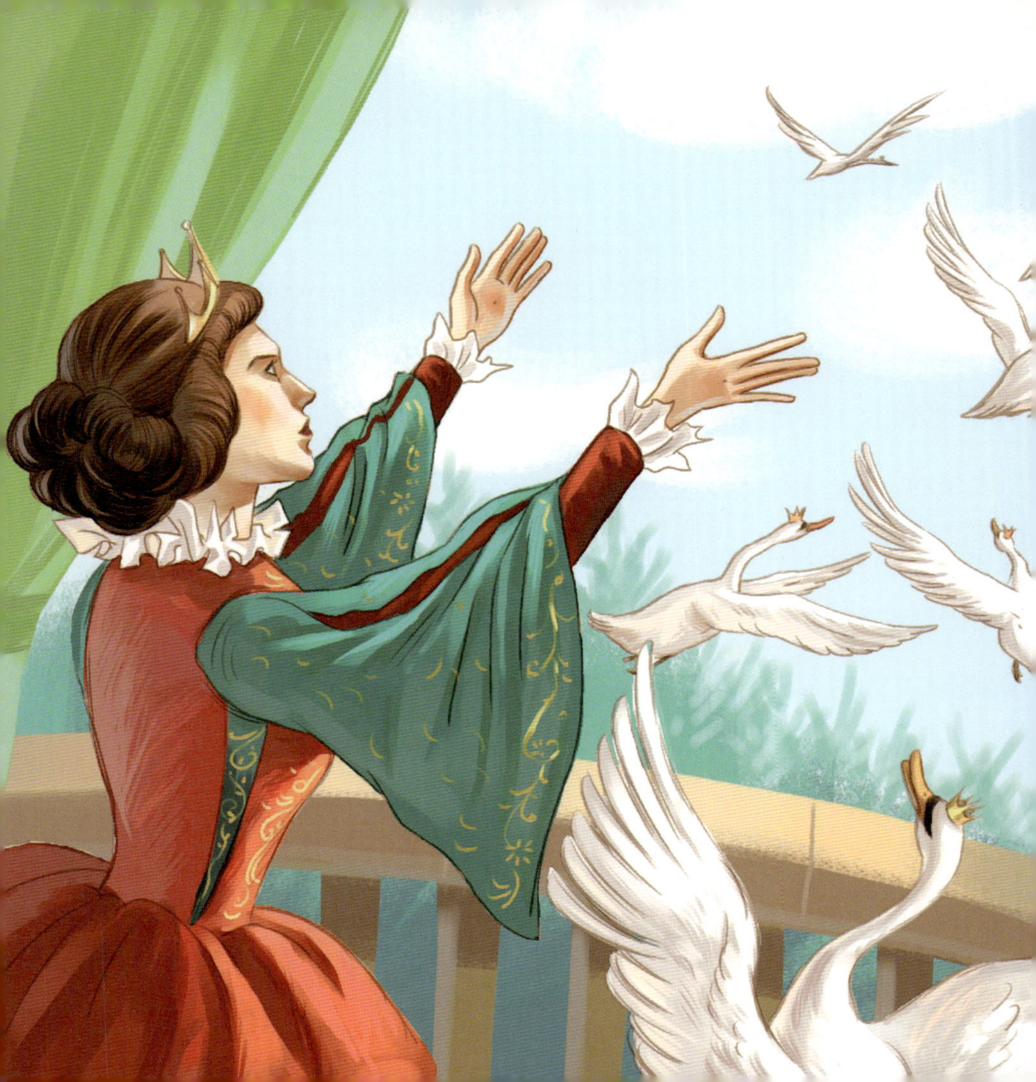

Elisa had to live in a very small house. She was very sad and lonely. But the story is not over[1] yet.

One day, 11 white swans came to Elisa's house. Elisa knew they were her brothers. "Come with us," they said. "We'll take you to a very distant place."

The swans carried Elisa. They flew for a long time. Finally, they came to a new country. Elisa was happy,

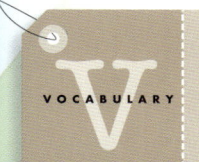

VOCABULARY

1. **over** adj. 終わって、おしまいになって

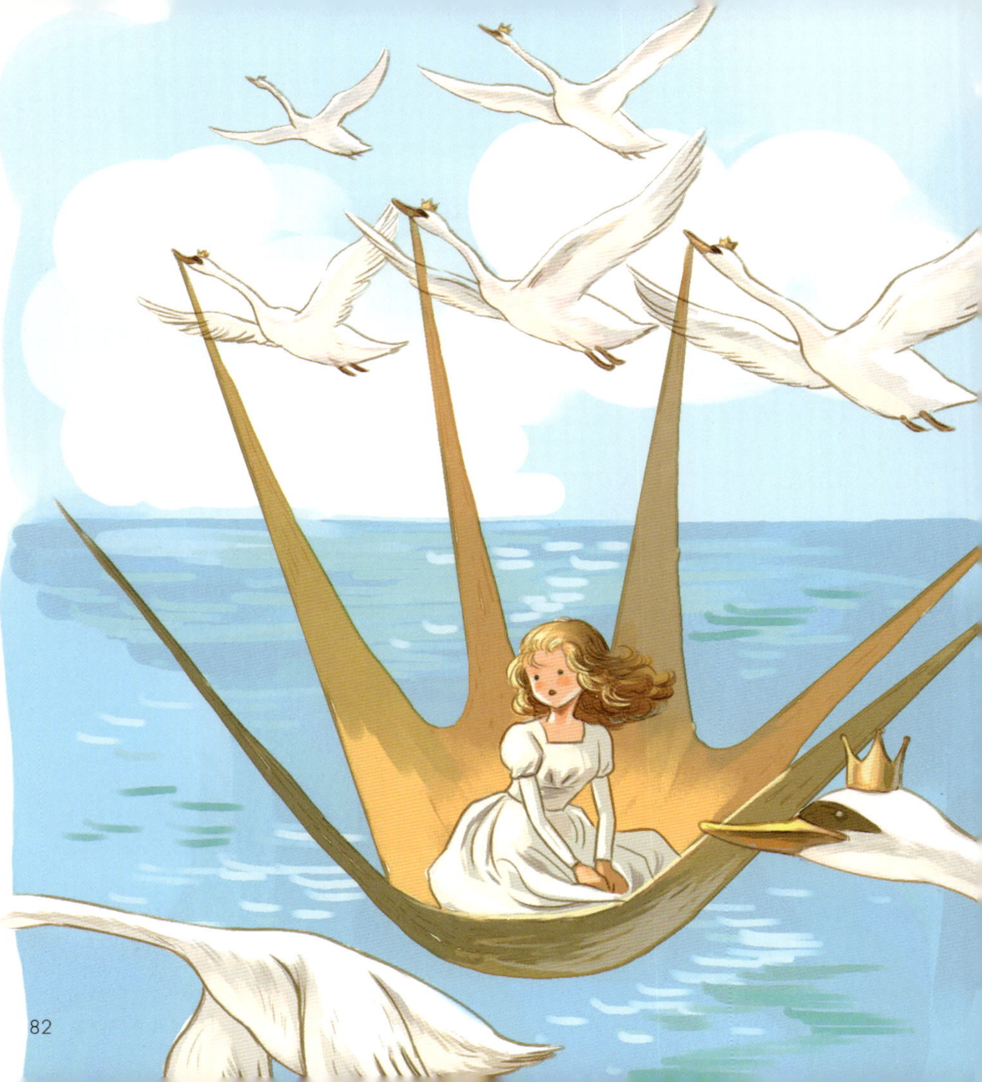

but she wanted to help her brothers. How could they become people again?

One night, Elisa saw a fairy. "You can help your brothers," said the fairy. "You must make 11 magic shirts. Then, your brothers must wear[1] them."

Elisa began to make the shirts. As she was working, a young king from another country saw her magic. "She's a

VOCABULARY

1. **wear** v. (wear-wore-worn) ☞ 着る

witch," the king thought. "We must kill**❶** her!"

The king took Elisa to the castle, but she kept working on**❷** the shirts. Later, a guard**❸** came to her. "Now you will die," he said. As they took Elisa outside, she finished the last shirt. 11 swans flew to her. She gave each one a shirt. They all became men again.

The young king was surprised. He and Elisa got married, and she became the queen.

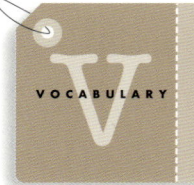

VOCABULARY
1. **kill** v. ☞ 殺す、始末する
2. **work on** v. ☞ 〜に取り組む
3. **guard** n. ☞ 守衛

ワイルドスワン | 85

訳：ワイルドスワン

これはとても遠い国のお話です。この国の王様と王妃には、11人の息子と1人の娘がいました。息子たちはとてもハンサムでした。1人娘の名前はエリザと言いました。そんなある日、王妃が亡くなりました。

その後、王様は新しい妻を見つけました。しかし、新しい妃はひどい悪人でした。彼女は王様の子どもたちを嫌い、魔法を使って11人の息子たちを真っ白な白鳥に変えてしまいました。そして、エリザを城から追い出しました。

エリザはとても小さな家で暮らさなくてはいけませんでした。エリザはとても悲しく、淋しい思いをしました。しかし、お話はここで終わりません。

ある日、11羽の白鳥がエリザの家にやって来ました。エリザには白鳥たちが兄弟であることがわかりました。「僕たちと一緒に行こう」と白鳥たちは言いました。「お前をとても遠い場所に連れて行くよ」

白鳥たちはエリザを運びました。長い間、飛び続け、ついに新しい国にたどり着きました。エリザは幸せでしたが、兄弟たちを助

けたいと考えました。どうすれば、彼らを人間に戻すことができるのでしょうか。

　ある夜、エリザは妖精を見ました。妖精は「兄弟たちを助けることはできますよ」と言いました。「11枚の魔法のシャツをお作りなさい。そして兄弟たちにそれを着せるのです」

　エリザはシャツを作り始めました。作業をしていると、別の国からやって来た若い王様がエリザの魔法を目にします。「彼女は魔女だ」と王様は考えました。「始末せねば！」

　王様はエリザを城に連れていきました。しかしエリザはシャツを作り続けました。その後、守衛が彼女のところにやってきます。「さぁ、お前はもう終わりだ」と守衛は言いました。外に連れ出されたとき、エリザは最後のシャツを仕上げました。11羽の白鳥はエリザのもとに飛んできました。エリザは1羽1羽にシャツを与えました。兄弟たちは皆、再び人間になりました。

　若い王様は驚きました。王様はエリザと結婚し、エリザは王妃になりました。

The Darning Needle
かがり針

This is the story of a cook and her darning needle.❶ Every day the needle admired herself.❷ She smiled and thought, "Look at how slender❸ and beautiful I am!"

The needle did not like the cook's fingers. They were so ugly! "You must be gentle with me," she said to them. "I am so delicate④ and pretty."

However, the cook's foolish fingers were too clumsy.⑤ They broke the needle into two pieces! The cook fixed the needle, and pinned⑥ it to her blouse. "Of course the cook wants to keep me," thought the needle. "After all, I am one of a kind!"

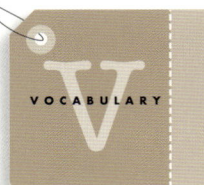

VOCABULARY

1. **darning needle** n. ☞ かがり針
2. **admire oneself** v. ☞ うぬぼれる
3. **slender** adj. ☞ スマートな、ほっそりした
4. **delicate** adj. ☞ 繊細な、壊れやすい
5. **clumsy** adj. ☞ 不器用な
6. **pin** v. ☞ 固定する

The needle was happy on the cook's blouse. Everyone could see her and admire her beauty. Then, while the cook was washing dishes, the needle fell from her blouse. It went down the drain.❶

"I am going to have an adventure,"❷ thought the needle. "Wonderful! I am too pretty to stay inside."

The needle went through a pipe❸ and landed on the street. She saw trash❹ everywhere. There was a stick,❺

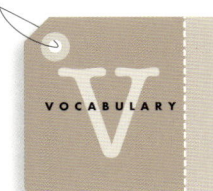

VOCABULARY

1. **drain** n. ☞ 下水管
2. **adventure** n. ☞ 冒険
3. **pipe** n. ☞ 管
4. **trash** n. ☞ ごみ
5. **stick** n. ☞ 小枝

a newspaper, and a straw.❶ The needle smiled. "Ha! I am more beautiful than they are!"

The needle saw a piece of glass in the middle of the street. It was shining very brightly.❷ "Excuse me," asked the needle. "Are you a diamond?"❸

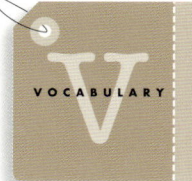

VOCABULARY

1. **straw** n. ☞ ストロー
2. **brightly** adv. ☞ 輝いて
3. **diamond** n. ☞ ダイヤモンド

The Darning Needle **かがり針** | 93

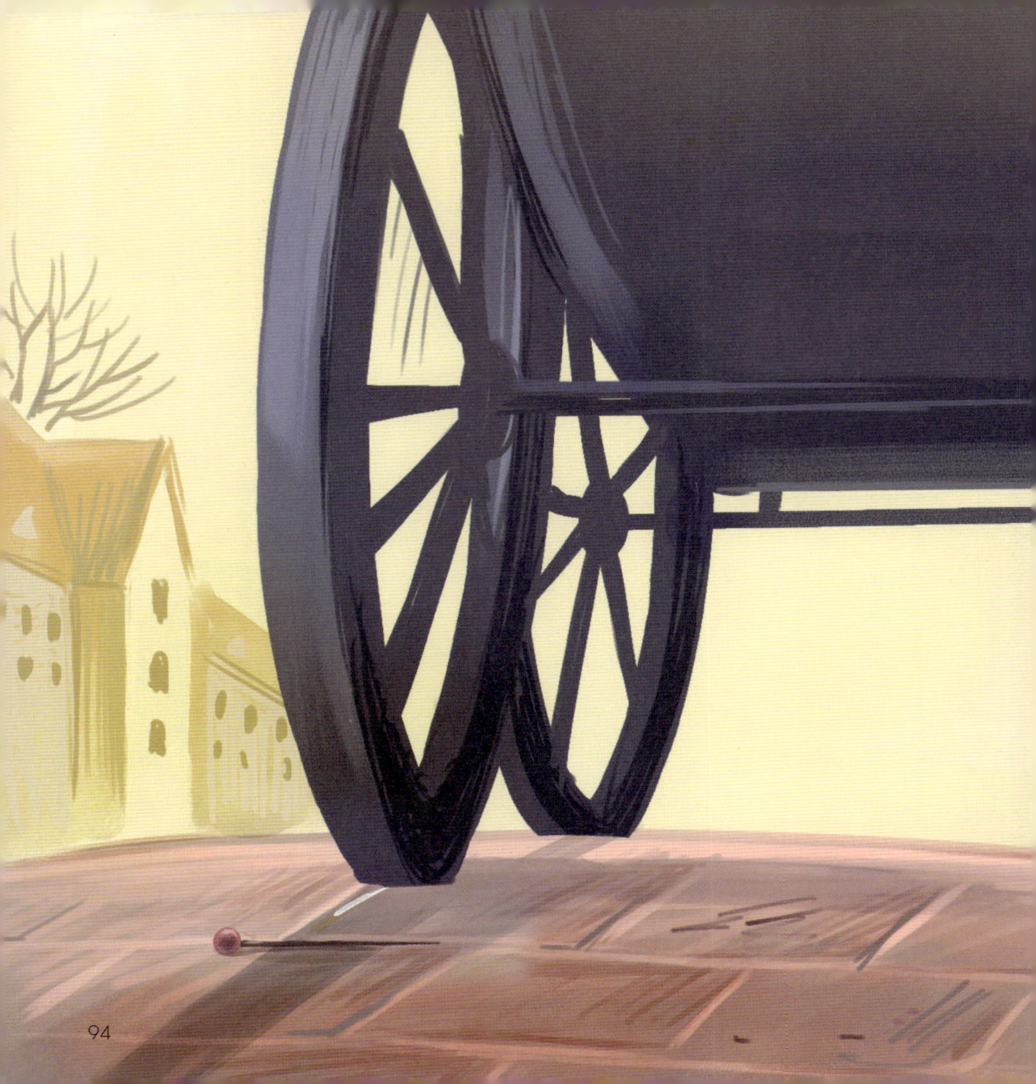

"I am something like that," answered the piece of glass. The two friends talked for a long time. They agreed that everyone else was foolish and impolite.❶ Why did nobody appreciate❷ their importance?❸

Suddenly, a heavy wagon❹ ran over❺ the needle. "I am broken," thought the needle. But the needle was not broken. She stayed in the street, and that is where the story ends.

VOCABULARY
1. **impolite** adj. ☞ 無礼な、失礼な
2. **appreciate** v. ☞ 感謝する
3. **importance** n. ☞ 重要性
4. **wagon** n. ☞ 荷馬車
5. **run over** v. ☞ 〜の上を走る、車でひく

訳：かがり針

　これは、料理人と料理人のかがり針の話です。針は、毎日自分を見てほれぼれしていました。針は笑みを浮かべながら思うのです。「こんなにスマートで美しい私。見てちょうだい！」

　針は料理人の指が嫌いでした。指たちはとても醜かったからです。「私にやさしくしないとダメよ」と針は指たちに言いました。「私はとても繊細で、きれいなんだから」

　しかし、料理人の愚かな指たちはあまりに不器用でした。指たちは、針を2つに折ってしまったのです！　料理人は針を直して、ブラウスに止めました。「当然、料理人は私を手元に置いておきたいのよね」と針は思いました。「いずれにしろ、私は唯一絶対の存在だから！」

　針は料理人のブラウスの上で幸せでした。皆が針を眺め、その美しさを愛でられるのですから。その後、料理人が皿を洗っている間、針はブラウスから落ちてしまいました。針は排水管を流れていきました。

「これから冒険が始まるのね」と針は考えました。「素敵！　家の中に留まるには私は美しすぎるのよ」

　針は管を流れ出て、道路の上に着きました。辺り一面ゴミだらけでした。棒切れや新聞紙、ストローがありました。針は微笑みました。「ハハ！　あいつらより私のほうがきれいだわ！」

　針は通りの真ん中にガラスの破片があるのを見つけました。それはとても明るく輝いていました。「すみませんけど」と針は尋ねました。「あなたはダイヤモンド？」

　「そのようなものだね」とガラスの破片は答えました。針とガラスは長い間話をしました。そして、自分たちの他は皆愚かで無作法だということで意見が一致しました。なぜ、誰も自分たちが大事な存在であることを認めないのか、と。

　突然、重い荷馬車が針の上を走っていきました。「壊れちゃったわ」と針は思いました。でも、針は壊れていません。針はまだ通りにいました。この話はここでおしまいです。

The Hardy
Tin Soldier

ブリキの兵隊

As the birthday present was opened, a tin[1] soldier heard a childlike[2] shout.[3] He and twenty-four other tin soldiers were a gift to a little boy. However, not all of them were complete.[4] One of the soldiers had only one leg.

After playing, the boy put his soldiers away near the other toys. The soldier saw a beautiful dancer[5] wearing a paper dress in a toy castle.

VOCABULARY

1. **tin** adj. ☞ ブリキ板で作った、ブリキの
2. **childlike** adj. ☞ 子どもらしい、子どものような
3. **shout** n. ☞ 叫び声
4. **complete** adj. ☞ 完全な、全部そろった
5. **dancer** n. ☞ ダンサー、踊る人

Her leg was lifted so high that it seemed she also had only one leg. The tin soldier fell in love with her at once.

One day, the boy placed the tin soldier to guard❶ an

open window. A strong wind pulled the soldier out. He tumbled[2] to the sidewalk. Although the boy and his mother searched, they couldn't find him.

VOCABULARY

1. **guard** v. ☞ 見張る、監視する
2. **tumble** v. ☞ 落ちる、落下する

102

The soldier was alone and covered by dirt.❶ Later, other children picked him up. They put him in a paper boat in a small stream,❷ which flowed into❸ a lake.

Suddenly, a fish jumped and swallowed him. He was nervous, but the thought of seeing the dancer again helped him to stay strong.

The soldier was deep inside the fish. Then sunlight burst

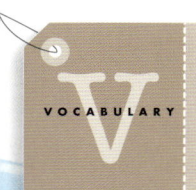

VOCABULARY
1. **dirt** n. ☞ ほこり、泥
2. **stream** n. ☞ 小川
3. **flow into** v. ☞ 〜に流れ込む

in.❶ He saw steam❷ coming from a teapot he recognized.❸ He was back in the boy's kitchen!

The soldier looked upon the dancer with joy. Suddenly, a cat struck the soldier and he fell into a pan in the oven. He watched the dancer sadly as he melted away.❹

Then a strong wind blew the dancer inside with him. She burned up in a flash.❺ Later, when the little boy looked, all he found inside was a tiny tin heart.

VOCABULARY
1. **burst in** v. ☞ 突然入ってくる
2. **steam** n. ☞ 蒸気
3. **recognize** v. ☞ 〜だとわかる
4. **melt away** v. ☞ 溶けてなくなる
5. **in a flash** ☞ すぐに

The Hardy Tin Soldier **ブリキの兵隊** | 105

訳：ブリキの兵隊

　誕生日プレゼントが開けられたとき、ブリキの兵隊は子どもの歓声を耳にしました。彼と24のブリキの兵隊は小さな少年への贈り物だったのです。でも、全員が完璧だったわけではありません。1人の兵隊には足が1本しかありませんでした。

　遊び終えると、少年はほかのおもちゃの近くに兵隊たちを片付けてしまいました。兵隊はおもちゃの城の中に、紙のドレスを着た美しい踊り子を見つけました。

　踊り子の足は高く上げられていたため、まるで彼女も1本の足しかないように見えました。ブリキの兵隊は一目で恋をしてしまいました。

　ある日、少年は、開いた窓の見張りとしてブリキの兵隊を置きました。しかし強い風に吹かれて外に投げ出された兵隊は、歩道に転がってしまいました。少年と母親が探しましたが、見つけることはできませんでした。

兵隊はひとりぼっちでほこりまみれ。よその子どもたちがその兵隊を拾い上げ、紙の船に乗せて小川に流しました。船は湖に流れ出ました。

　突然、魚がジャンプし、兵隊を飲み込んでしまいます。兵隊は不安でしたが、踊り子にもう一度会うんだという思いが気持ちを強くしてくれました。

　兵隊は魚の体奥深くにいました。すると、太陽の光が急に差し込みました。ティーポットから蒸気が上がっているのを見て兵隊は理解しました。少年の家の台所に帰ってきたのです！

　兵隊は喜んで踊り子を見上げました。突然、猫に体当たりされてオーブンの中の皿に落ちてしまいます。兵隊は、溶けながら悲しげに踊り子を見つめました。

　すると、強い風が吹いて踊り子が兵隊の上に落ちてきました。踊り子はあっという間に燃えてしまいました。後で少年が見ると、そこにはハートの形をした小さなブリキだけが残っていました。

Index

索引

A

- a long time ago ··············52
- aboard ···············31
- admire oneself ···············90
- adventure ···············91
- all along ···············35
- all by oneself ···············49
- aloud ···············35
- appreciate ···············95
- attractive ···············59
- awful ···············73

B

- barely ···············73
- be covered in ···············49
- be covered with ···············22
- belong to ···············32
- black and blue ···············73
- blow ···············49
- branch ···············42
- brightly ···············92
- bring tears to one's eyes ········21
- burst in ··············104
- bury ···············64

C

- cage ···············63
- capture ···············60
- careless ···············63
- ceiling ···············73
- chase ···············60
- cherish ···············44
- childlike ···············99
- chop ~ into ···············44
- clumsy ···············90
- comfort ···············63
- comfortable ···············44
- complain ···············73

complete	99
concern	64
countryside	59
cure	25

D

daisy	59
dancer	99
darning needle	90
decoration	42
delicate	90
delicious	52
diamond	92
dirt	103
distant	32
doubtful	70
drain	91

F

faint	39
fairy	10
fear for	35
fir tree	39
flow into	103
fly	55

G

get away	13
grave	64
guard (n)	84
guard (v)	101

H

handsome	79
hang	42
high in the sky	55
hug oneself	51
huge	31

I

impolite	95
importance	95
in a flash	104
in return for	13
indoors	49

instead	60	**O**	
J		on top	72
just like	22	one's people	31
K		over	81
kill	84	**P**	
L		pass away	79
light	52	pass out	32
live happily ever after	74	path	59
look after	13	pea	72
lovelier	19	petal	59
M		pin	90
marvelous	25	pipe	91
mattress	72	pity	63
mechanical	22	place	42
melt away	104	plain	19
mess	70	pond	13
mole	13	pot	10
N		potion	31
nearby	39	prepare	52
		prevent	35

put away ……………………25	

R

recognize …………………… 104	
reject ………………………69	
remain ……………………22	
run over ……………………95	

S

seek …………………………31	
sensitive…………………… 74	
shell …………………………31	
shine …………………………22	
shout …………………………99	
slender ……………………90	
stay warm …………………51	
steam ……………………… 104	
stick …………………………91	
straw ………………………92	
stream …………………… 103	
swallow ……………………32	
swan …………………………79	

T

terrible ……………………69	
terribly……………………39	
the king of ~ ……………… 15	
tin ……………………………99	
tiny …………………………10	
toad…………………………10	
together ……………………55	
toss and turn………………73	
trash ………………………91	
treasure ……………………25	
tumble …………………… 101	

U

ugly …………………………10	
upstairs ……………………42	

W

wagon………………………95	
wander around ……………72	
wear ………………………83	
wooden ……………………64	
work on ……………………84	

Live ABC

　株式会社 Live ABC は、台湾の e-Learning プログラムにおいてトップレベルの実績を誇っている大手出版社です。最先端の IT 技術と経験豊富な技術者と語学教師及び編集スタッフによって、インタラクティブマルチメディア語学学習教材の研究開発に取り組んでいます。
　現在、英語を筆頭に中国語、日本語、韓国語などの語学学習教材を、書籍や、CD-ROM、スマートフォン対応のアプリで提供しています。

ホームページ（英語）：http://www.liveabc.com

カバーデザイン	土岐 晋二（d-fractal）
本文デザイン／DTP	土岐 晋二（d-fractal）
英文翻訳	佐藤 淳子
CD ナレーション	Jack Merluzzi
	Carolyn Miller
	友丘 真佐江

音読 CD BOOK ⑦
やさしい英語で読む　アンデルセン童話　〜 Andersen's Fairy Tales 〜　BEST 10
平成 24 年（2012 年）　11 月 10 日　　初版第 1 刷発行
平成 28 年（2016 年）　10 月 10 日　　　　　第 2 刷発行

編　者　Live ABC
発行人　福田富与
発行所　有限会社 J リサーチ出版
　　　　〒166-0002　東京都杉並区高円寺北 2-29-14-705
　　　　電話 03 (6808) 8801（代）　FAX 03 (5364) 5310
　　　　編集部 03 (6808) 8806
　　　　http://www.jresearch.co.jp
印刷所　（株）シナノ パブリッシング プレス

ISBN978-4-86392-122-1　禁無断転載。なお、乱丁・落丁はお取り替えいたします。
Copyright ©2012 LiveABC Interactive Corporation
Japanese translation copyright ©2012 J-Research Press, Japanese edition. All Rights Reserved.